The Inside Guide

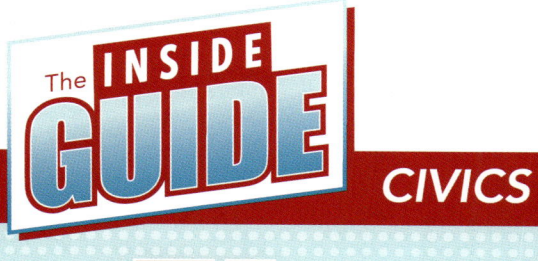

CIVICS

Elections

By Cassie M. Lawton

Cavendish Square

New York

Published in 2021 by Cavendish Square Publishing, LLC
243 5th Avenue, Suite 136, New York, NY 10016

Copyright © 2021 by Cavendish Square Publishing, LLC

First Edition

No part of this publication may be reproduced, stored in a retrieval system, or transmitted in any form or by any means—electronic, mechanical, photocopying, recording, or otherwise—without the prior permission of the copyright owner. Request for permission should be addressed to Permissions, Cavendish Square Publishing, 243 5th Avenue, Suite 136, New York, NY 10016. Tel (877) 980-4450; fax (877) 980-4454.

Website: cavendishsq.com

This publication represents the opinions and views of the author based on his or her personal experience, knowledge, and research. The information in this book serves as a general guide only. The author and publisher have used their best efforts in preparing this book and disclaim liability rising directly or indirectly from the use and application of this book.

All websites were available and accurate when this book was sent to press.

Portions of this work were originally authored by Leslie Harper and published as *How Do Elections Work? (Civics Q&A)*. All new material this edition authored by Cassie M. Lawton.

Library of Congress Cataloging-in-Publication Data

Names: Lawton, Cassie M., author.
Title: Elections / by Cassie M. Lawton.
Description: First edition. | New York, NY : Cavendish Square Publishing, 2021. |
Series: The inside guide. Civics | Includes index.
Identifiers: LCCN 2019059489 (print) | LCCN 2019059490 (ebook) |
ISBN 9781502657039 (library binding) | ISBN 9781502657015 (paperback) |
ISBN 9781502657022 (set) | ISBN 9781502657046 (ebook)
Subjects: LCSH: Elections–United States–Juvenile literature. |
Voting–United States–Juvenile literature.
Classification: LCC JK1978 .L38 2021 (print) | LCC JK1978 (ebook) |
DDC 324.60973–dc23
LC record available at https://lccn.loc.gov/2019059489
LC ebook record available at https://lccn.loc.gov/2019059490

Editor: Kristen Susienka
Copy Editor: Nathan Heidelberger
Designer: Tanya Dellaccio

The photographs in this book are used by permission and through the courtesy of: Cover Drew Angerer/Getty Images News/Getty Images; pp. 4, 6, 12, 22 Hill Street Studios/DigitalVision/Getty Images; p. 7 Image Source/Photodisc/Getty Images; p. 8 (top) DEA / G. NIMATALLAH/De Agostini via Getty Images; p. 8 (bottom) SDI Productions/E+/Getty Images; p. 9 Library of Congress/Corbis/VCG via Getty Images; p. 10 EMMANUEL DUNAND/AFP via Getty Images; p. 13 Scott Heins/Getty Images; p. 14 Tero Vesalainen/Shutterstock.com; p. 15 Martina Albertazzi/Bloomberg via Getty Images; pp. 16, 29 (top) ANDREW CABALLERO-REYNOLDS/AFP via Getty Images; pp. 18–19 Whitney Curtis/Getty Images; p. 19 Mark Wilson/Getty Images; p. 20 Michele Eve Sandberg/Corbis via Getty Images; p. 21 Encyclopaedia Britannica/Universal Images Group via Getty Images; p. 24 Ariel Skelley/DigitalVision/Getty Images; p. 26 RomanR/Shutterstock.com; p. 27 fstop123/E+/Getty Images; p. 28 (top) https://upload.wikimedia.org/wikipedia/commons/b/b6/Gilbert_Stuart_Williamstown_Portrait_of_George_Washington.jpg; p. 28 (bottom) Evan El-Amin/Shutterstock.com; p. 29 (middle) Daniel Acker/Bloomberg via Getty Images; p. 29 (bottom) Dirk Anschutz/Stone/Getty Images.

Some of the images in this book illustrate individuals who are models. The depictions do not imply actual situations or events.

CPSIA compliance information: Batch #CS20CSQ: For further information contact Cavendish Square Publishing LLC, New York, New York, at 1-877-980-4450.

Printed in the United States of America

Find us on

CONTENTS

Chapter One: 5
    Elections: What Are They?

Chapter Two: 11
    Understanding Political Parties

Chapter Three: 17
    Election Day

Chapter Four: 23
    Voting Is a Right

Timeline: 28
    Key US Presidential Elections

Think About It! 29

Glossary 30

Find Out More 31

Index 32

Voting is a right that not everyone in the world has. It's important to vote once you're old enough.

ELECTIONS: WHAT ARE THEY?

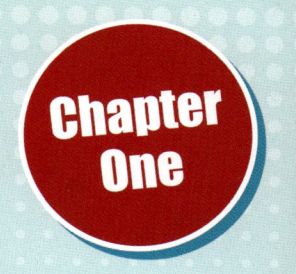

Chapter One

Imagine you're with some friends. You want to go to a movie, but you can't agree on which one. You decide to take a vote. Friends raise their hands for different movies. In the end, the movie with the most raised hands, or votes, wins. Voting is an easy way to find out what most of the people in a group want. It's also an important part of being a citizen.

Types of Elections

When people vote on who will be in charge of something, it's called an election. You may have voted in a student council election at your school. Elections are held for many of the positions in local, state, and national governments. Understanding how elections work can help you make smart decisions when it's time to cast your vote!

There are several types of elections. Some examples are primary elections, general elections, and special elections.

In a primary election, members of a certain group vote to choose the person who will be that group's candidate in the larger general election that follows. The winner of the general election takes office for a certain amount of time, called a term.

Candidates work hard to win the votes of people in their communities.

For example, US citizens vote for a president every four years. Members of the US **House of Representatives** serve for two-year terms. Senators in the United States are elected every six years. Sometimes a person can't serve for a full term. When that happens, a special election is often held to fill the job until the next general election.

Learning About Candidates

Being an informed citizen is an important part of voting in elections. It's good to learn as much as possible about the candidates running for office—another word for a government position—before Election Day. Voters have the opportunity to learn more about different candidates by visiting their websites and social media accounts or by attending events called town hall meetings and rallies. They can learn about a candidate's **political party**, their background, and their plans for the future before they exercise their right to vote.

School elections teach students about voting.

Who Votes?

Voting has been around for a long time in many different civilizations, but not everyone has always been able to vote. In the past, only certain people could vote in elections. For a long time, white men were the only people who could vote in the United States. African Americans, Native Americans, women, and other people spent many years fighting for the right to vote. To vote today, you need only to be a US citizen and at least 18 years old.

Before voting, a person must register with the local **board of elections**. Registering lets the government know who you are and where you live. That way, you can vote in the right city,

Fast Fact

A 1924 law gave Native Americans the right to vote, though some states didn't allow them to vote until much later.

7

Fast Fact
One of the first civilizations to hold elections was ancient Greece.

ancient Greek ballots

county, and state elections. Registering also keeps an election fair by making sure no one votes more than once.

When you vote, you sign in at a **polling place**. The sign-in sheet lists all the registered voters in a district, or the area of a city where you vote. Once you've signed in, it's time to vote. In some places, voting is done electronically, meaning you can touch buttons on a screen to cast your vote. In other places, people vote by filling out a form called a ballot with a pencil. Forms completed in this way are often fed into a machine that counts the votes.

Volunteers help voters through the voting process. Without them, voting might be very disorganized. It's important to thank volunteers for their time when you visit a polling place. They're an important part of our democracy!

Women couldn't vote in national elections in the United States until 1920.

THE RIGHTS OF WOMEN VOTERS

In the 1800s and early 1900s, American women worked hard to be given the right to vote. In the late 1800s, some parts of the country, especially Western places like Wyoming and Utah, began allowing women to vote. However, most American women were still denied their right to vote. Thousands of angry women on the East Coast and in other parts of the country held protests. Some women were arrested for trying to vote illegally. Any woman who wanted the right to vote was called a suffragette. That's because the right to vote is called suffrage. Leaders in the women's suffrage movement included Elizabeth Cady Stanton, Lucretia Mott, Ida B. Wells-Barnett, Alice Paul, and Susan B. Anthony. Their efforts paid off. Women around the country were allowed to vote starting in 1920, which was when the 19th **Amendment** was added to the US Constitution.

Fast Fact
The United Kingdom also had a women's suffrage movement. Women living there couldn't vote until 1928.

Women worked tirelessly to gain the right to vote.

US presidents are often a symbol of their political party. For example, President Barack Obama was a symbol of the Democratic Party.

UNDERSTANDING POLITICAL PARTIES

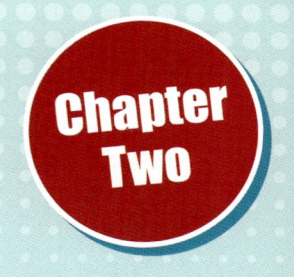

Chapter Two

Political parties play an important part in elections in the United States. Although people don't have to vote for the candidates from their political party in a general election, they often support their party's candidates. Each political party has its own ideas about what the government should do. Sometimes, different political parties have ideas that are very different from each other, and this can cause tension.

Why Have Them?

Many people have different ideas about how the government should work. A group of people with similar ideas may join or form a political party that **promotes** those ideas. Members of a party don't always agree on everything. However, knowing what political party candidates belong to can often give you a general idea of what they believe.

In the United States, the two major political parties are the Democratic Party and the Republican Party. There will usually be a Democratic and Republican candidate in each election. Sometimes candidates from smaller parties run too. Some candidates, called Independents, do not belong to any party.

Symbols of the Republican Party include the color red and an elephant. Democrats are connected to the color blue and the donkey.

Two Main Parties

The Democratic Party and the Republican Party have a long history. Their names have been part of US elections since the 1800s. However, their ideas have changed over time. Today, Democratic Party members believe the national government should play an active role in people's lives by doing things like providing **universal health care** and helping make college more affordable. They often consider **environmental** issues very important too. On the other hand, the Republican Party generally has

Fast Fact
The first US president, George Washington, didn't like political parties because he thought they would bring more division to the country rather than bring people together.

Fast Fact
Rallies are held to support a candidate or a political party.

Bernie Sanders is an Independent and a Democrat. He ran for president as a Democrat in 2020.

more **conservative** views, especially on social issues. Many Republicans believe in limiting the power of the national government and letting states make many of their own decisions.

How to Decide

When someone is elected into office, they'll be making important decisions. That's why it's smart to research the candidates and their political parties before an election. This can give you clues about what they plan to do if they're elected.

Start by reading about a candidate and the party they belong to. Do you agree with what the candidate and that party stand for? You can also

Fast Fact
The Green Party is another, smaller political party in the United States. Its members often support environmentally friendly, or "green," actions and policies, as well as more liberal ideals.

make a list of the issues that are important to you. Do some research, and find out what the candidate thinks about each issue.

Some of the best places to turn to are a candidate's website and social media accounts. You can learn more about them through their posts. However, make sure to read information about each candidate carefully, especially if you're reading online articles. Today, many fake news articles are shared on the internet. Also, different websites support different political parties, so they might not always be fair and balanced. Check facts against other articles from trusted sources. Ask trusted adults to help you too. It's important to always be informed about candidates.

Many politicians, such as President Donald Trump, are on social media. Get a parent or guardian's permission before going online to learn more about them.

DEBATES

Discussions called debates are held before many elections. They give candidates the chance to talk to the public and each other about their ideas and values. It's an opportunity for voters to see the candidates talking about important issues side by side.

Presidential debates are often shown on TV. Televised presidential debates have been happening in the United States since 1960. Today, presidential debates are watched by millions of people. They help voters choose a candidate for a primary or general election.

However, debates don't just happen between members of major political parties or national candidates. They can happen in your school too. Candidates for student council might hold a debate before an election. At the debate, you can learn about what the kids running for class president plan to do. This can help you choose whom to vote for when the time comes.

Fast Fact

John F. Kennedy and Richard Nixon were the candidates who took part in America's first televised presidential debate in 1960.

Debates give voters the opportunity to compare candidates directly.

People often line up to vote on Election Day in their community.

ELECTION DAY

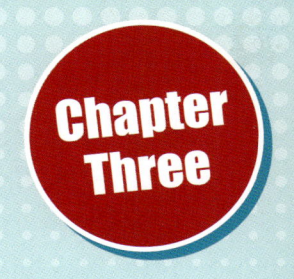

Chapter Three

People in the United States can vote for many different leaders, such as mayor, governor, senator, representative, and president. Different elections can be held at different times during the year. However, national elections are held on the first Tuesday of November (or the second Tuesday, if November begins on a Tuesday). This day is called Election Day, and it's an exciting time in the United States.

At the Polls

On Election Day, it's important that every registered voter has a chance to vote. Voters go to a polling place, which is where they cast their votes in local, state, and national elections. Polling places are set up in schools, community centers, and other places that people can easily get to. A person's polling place is often close to where they live. Most polling places open early in the morning and close late in the evening. This gives people who work different hours time to get to a polling place.

At the polling place, each person marks his or her vote on a form called a ballot. In the United States, citizens vote by secret ballot. That means that no one else knows for whom another person voted. At polling places, there are sometimes rows of voting booths. These booths allow voters to cast their votes in private.

Counting Votes

In a presidential election, millions of votes are cast in one day. Have you ever wondered how all of those votes are counted so quickly? Machines can do a lot of the counting for us.

In the past, many states used punch-card ballots. These ballots could be run through machines that counted the holes punched next to each candidate's name. Today, most states use paper ballots that are filled out by hand and then scanned by a machine. Electronic voting machines with touch screens are becoming more popular in the 21st century, although many people still like the idea of having paper ballots, in case something goes wrong with the machines.

There are different ways of voting, but each vote is collected once a person is finished and added to the overall **tally**. Ask an adult to take you with them when they vote so you can see the voting process in action.

Shown here is a sample Missouri ballot from Election Day in 2016.

Fast Fact
On Election Day, citizens are also often able to vote on laws and other plans for their community.

After the Electoral College meets, the US Congress counts their votes. The vice president leads this process.

The Electoral College

In local and state elections, the candidate with the most votes wins. However, US presidential elections are different. Within a state, each vote is counted. This is called the popular vote. Instead of voting for a candidate, though, citizens are really voting for people called electors. The political parties in a state choose electors. Then, the electors vote to decide which presidential candidate wins. This process is called the Electoral College.

The number of electors each state gets is equal to its number of senators and representatives. In some states, the electors must vote for the winner of the state's popular vote. In other states, the electors are free to vote for who they think is the best choice—often their party's candidate.

> **Fast Fact**
> People can also count scanned ballots by hand. This might be necessary if an election is very close and the number of votes needs to be double-checked.

OTHER TYPES OF BALLOTS

An American living in another country or outside the state where they are registered to vote can still make their voice heard. They can do this by filling out an **absentee ballot**, which they mail in to cast their vote. In addition, in many states, early voting is becoming more common. Through early voting, people can receive a regular ballot and send in their completed form before the actual election occurs. Not every state in the United States has this option, but if you know someone who's going to vote, check out your state's voting rules. If they can vote early, encourage them to do so! These methods make it easier for people to vote. Every vote matters, so having these other options is a great way to get more people to vote.

Once people send in their absentee ballots, they're sorted by voting district and added to the total count.

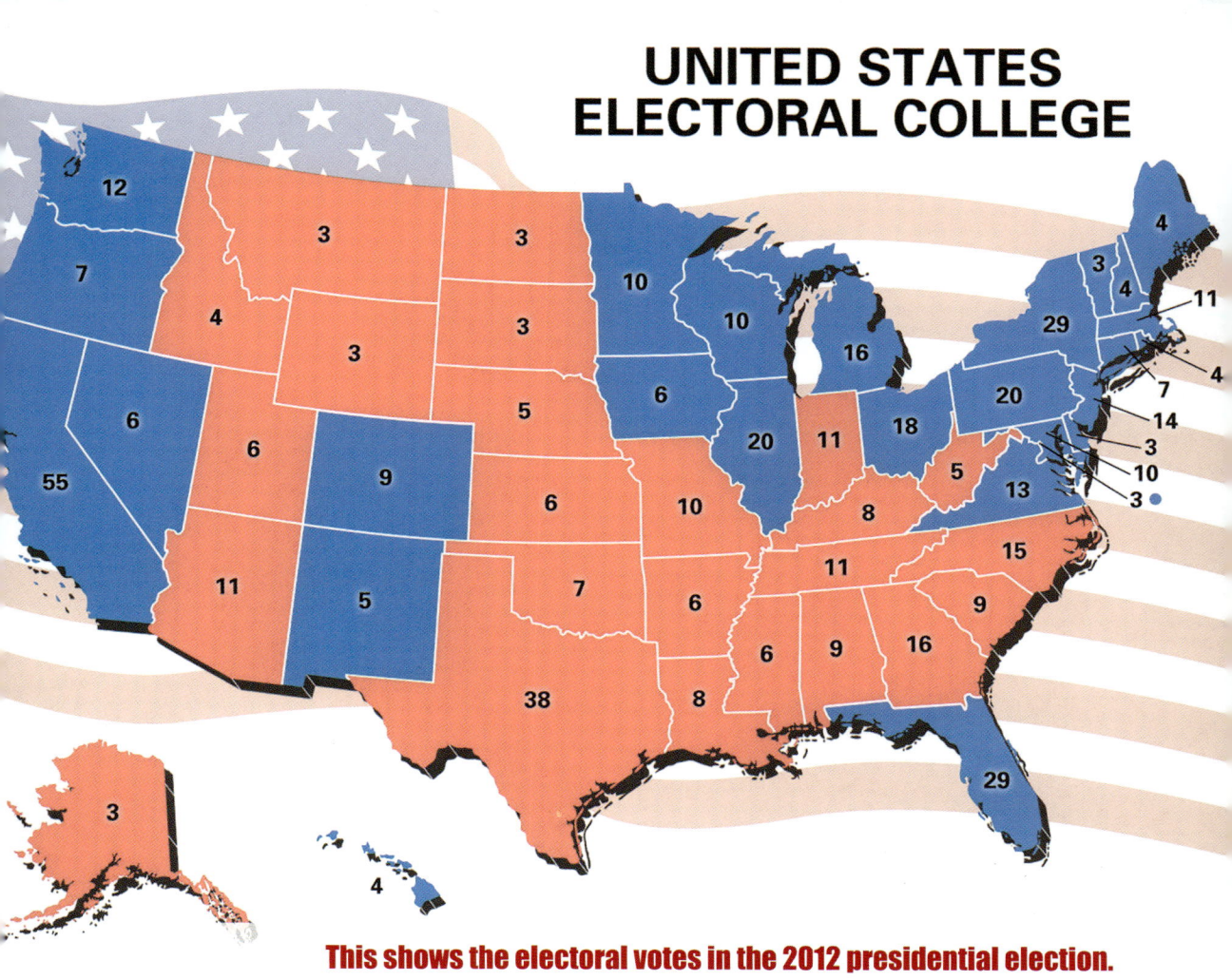

UNITED STATES ELECTORAL COLLEGE

This shows the electoral votes in the 2012 presidential election.

Fast Fact

Some people think the Electoral College shouldn't exist anymore. They say it causes confusion and doesn't always represent the people's choice. This is because a candidate can win the popular vote but lose in the Electoral College. A candidate needs 270 electoral votes out of 538 to win an election.

21

Voting is an important part of active citizenship.

VOTING IS A RIGHT

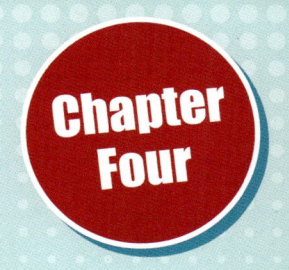

Chapter Four

All adult US citizens have the right to vote. It's a right that should not be taken for granted and should be exercised whenever possible. Even though kids can't vote, they can look to the example of others who can to prepare for their future as active citizens.

Always remember that voting in elections is a big responsibility. When you become an adult, voting will be a great way to make your voice heard. However, you're never too young to take part in an election!

How to Help

One way you can help others make a decision is by investigating the candidates they need to choose from. If you do your own research about a candidate, you can be better informed. Using the information you find, you can choose a candidate to support. Then, you can share information about this candidate with others. You can make signs and posters telling people why they should vote for that person. You can also encourage people to vote. Reminding the adults in your life of their responsibility as US citizens to vote is a great way to be involved in elections even if you can't vote yet.

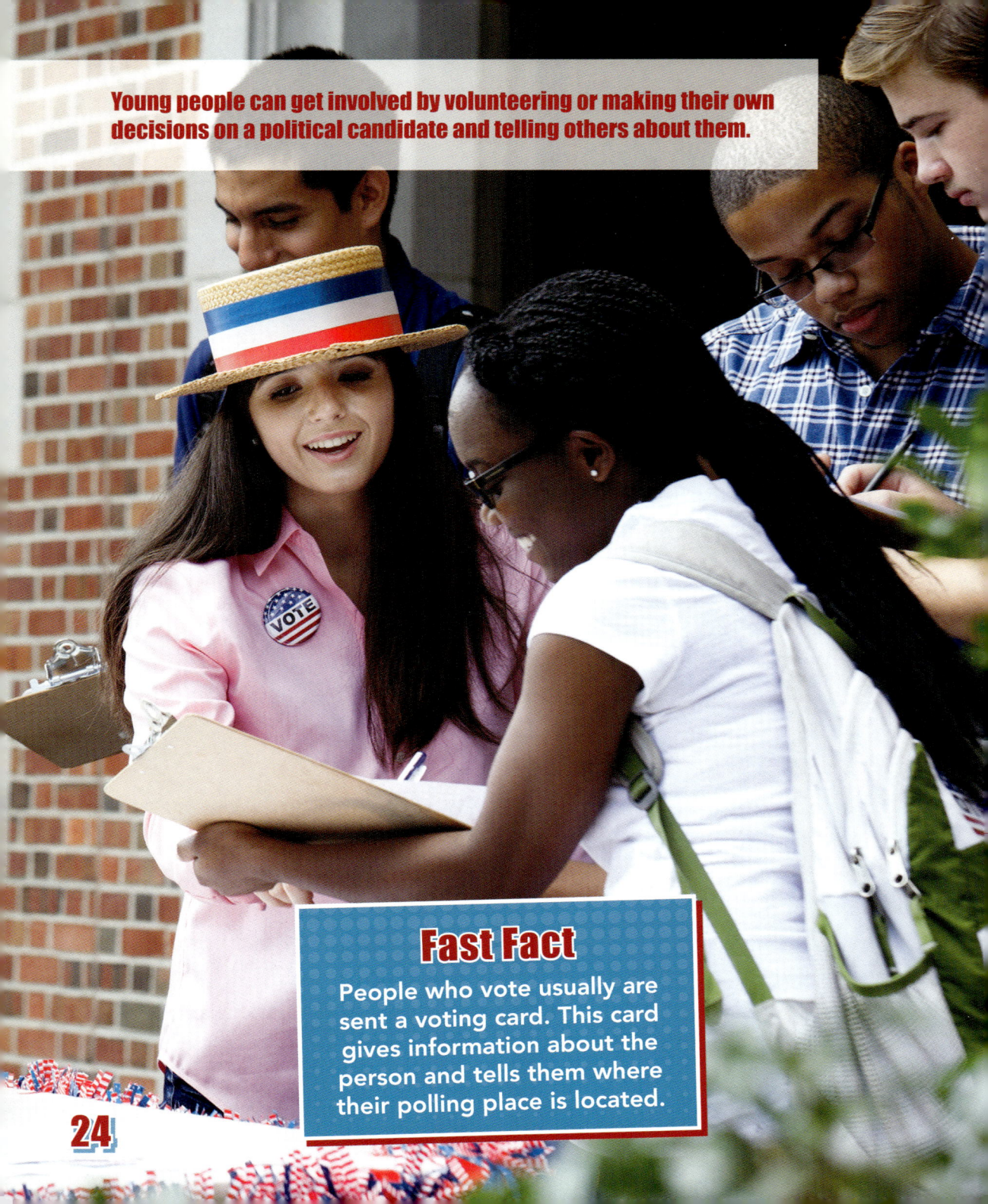

Young people can get involved by volunteering or making their own decisions on a political candidate and telling others about them.

Fast Fact

People who vote usually are sent a voting card. This card gives information about the person and tells them where their polling place is located.

You can also support a candidate in school elections. You can do many of the same things you'd do for a larger election. You can research a person you want to support. You can then talk to that person, attend school debates or speeches they're giving, and help them get their message out to others by being part of a campaign. You can make signs, posters, and stickers supporting your choice. You can tell others about your candidate's opinions and ideas. You could also run in a school election yourself!

If you decide that you want to run for office at your school or one day as an adult, remember that voting matters. It's important to get many people on your side to vote for you. Everything you do or say is important in an election. To get supporters, you should be honest and believe in your ideas and values. More people will listen to you and vote for you if they agree with you and believe you're a good person.

Fast Fact

While all citizens have the right to vote, that right usually goes away if a person is in jail. Once the person is out of jail, they can often register to vote again, but sometimes not until a few years later. In some states, however, people who were in jail for a serious crime are never allowed to vote again.

Each Vote Matters

Whether an election is big or small, every vote counts. Always remember that voting matters whether or not the people you voted for win the election. It's a chance to take part in making your voice heard in your school, community, or country. Sometimes elections are decided by just a few votes, so one person exercising their right to vote can make a big difference!

Voter Registration Application

Before completing this form, review the General, Application, and State specific...

Are you a citizen of the United States of America? ☐ Yes ☐ No
Will you be 18 years old on or before election day? ☐ Yes ☐ No
If you checked "No" in response to either of these questions, do not complete form.
(Please see state-specific instructions for rules regarding eligibility to register prior to age 18.)

This space for office use o...

1	☐ Mr. ☐ Miss ☐ Mrs. ☐ Ms.	Last Name	First Name
2	Home Address		Apt. or Lot #	City/Town
3	Address Where You Get Your Mail If Different From Above		City/Town
4	Date of Birth — Month / Day / Year	5	Telephone Number (optional)	6	ID Numb...
7	Choice of Party (see item 7 in the instructions for your State)	8	Race or Ethnic Group (see item 8 in the instructions for your State)

...state's instructions and I swear/affirm that:

Fast Fact

One way you can get involved is by helping at voter registration drives in your community. These are events where people help others register to vote.

POLL WORKERS

People who help set up and manage polling places are called poll workers. They're very important on Election Day. They help prepare everything a voter needs to vote correctly. Some of their responsibilities include setting up voting booths, making sure equipment is delivered to the correct place, managing voter **rosters**, and making sure all voting is done secretly. Poll workers might also help voters place their ballots in a ballot-reading machine. Most poll workers must be old enough to register to vote, but sometimes high school students can get involved. If this is something you'd like to do when you're older, keep this in mind!

Poll workers help voters on Election Day.

TIMELINE

Key US Presidential Elections

1789
The first US presidential election takes place. George Washington is elected without an opponent.

1800
In the first election to really show the bitter divisions between political parties, Thomas Jefferson is elected.

1860
In the first victory for the Republican Party, Abraham Lincoln wins the election. This outcome soon leads to the American Civil War.

1960
The first televised presidential debate takes place between John F. Kennedy and Richard Nixon.

2000
The election between George W. Bush and Al Gore results in a voting count dispute that has to be settled by the Supreme Court.

2008
The United States' first African American president, Barack Obama, is elected.

2016
Donald Trump defeats the first major-party female candidate, Hillary Clinton. Trump wins in the Electoral College, but Clinton wins the popular vote.

THINK ABOUT IT!

1. Why is it important to vote in elections?

2. Think about not being able to vote. How would you feel? How could you fight for the right to vote?

3. What type of voting method do you think you'd like best? Why?

4. What is the Electoral College, and what role does it play in presidential elections? Do you think it's needed or not? Why?

5. What are some ways you can get involved in elections even if you can't vote in them?

29

GLOSSARY

absentee ballot: A voting form sent to a person living outside a state or country so they can vote in elections.

amendment: A formal change to an official document, such as a constitution.

board of elections: A group of people who manage the election process for their community.

conservative: Upholding or supporting traditional or long-held beliefs in a political or social sense.

environmental: Relating to nature.

House of Representatives: A part of Congress, the lawmaking body of the US government.

political party: A group of people with similar beliefs about how the government should be run.

polling place: A place where people vote.

promote: To put forward in a positive light with hopes to win.

roster: A list of names.

tally: A count.

universal health care: The concept that health services should be affordable for and available to everyone.

FIND OUT MORE

Books
Gunderson, Jessica. *Understanding Your Role in Elections*. North Mankato, MN: Capstone Press, 2018.

Roberts, David. *Suffragette: The Battle for Equality*. London, UK: Walker Books, 2019.

Shamir, Ruby. *What's the Big Deal About Elections?* New York, NY: Philomel Books, 2018.

Websites
DK Find Out: What Is an Election?
www.dkfindout.com/us/more-find-out/what-does-politician-do/what-is-an-election
Explore all about elections at this informative website.

Kids Voting
kidsvotingusa.org
This website examines different ways kids can be educated about voting and become informed voters in the future.

Presidential Election Process
www.usa.gov/election
This website offers an explanatory video and article about the voting process in the United States.

Publisher's note to educators and parents: Our editors have carefully reviewed these websites to ensure that they are suitable for students. Many websites change frequently, however, and we cannot guarantee that a site's future contents will continue to meet our high standards of quality and educational value. Be advised that students should be closely supervised whenever they access the Internet.

INDEX

A
absentee ballots, 20

B
ballots, 8, 17, 18, 20, 27
board of elections, 7

C
criminals, 25

D
debates, 15, 25, 28
Democratic Party, 10, 11, 12

E
early voting, 20
Election Day, 6, 16, 17, 18, 20, 27
Electoral College, 19, 21
electronic voting, 8, 18

G
general elections, 5, 6, 11, 15

H
House of Representatives, 6, 17, 19

O
Obama, Barack, 10, 28

P
political parties, 6, 10, 11–14, 15, 19, 28
polling place, 8, 17, 24, 27
poll workers, 8, 27
popular vote, 19, 21
president, 6, 10, 12, 13, 14, 15, 17, 18, 19
primary elections, 5, 15

R
rallies, 6, 13
registration, 7–8, 20, 25, 26, 27
Republican Party, 11, 12–13, 28
research, 13–14, 23–25

S
school elections, 5, 7, 15, 19, 25
Senate, 6, 17, 19
social media, 6, 14, 23
special election, 5, 6

T
terms, 5–6
town hall meetings, 6
Trump, Donald, 14, 28

V
volunteers, 8, 24
voting booths, 17, 27
voting rights, 4, 7, 8, 9, 22, 23, 25

W
Washington, George, 12, 28